Compiled & Written by Amelia Riedler

Designed by Steve Potter

You've made a difference.

Every gift offers us a reason to be thankful. Every blessing presents us with the opportunity to appreciate the joys that can be found in each day. And every good person offers us the chance to recognize good things that are already present in our lives.

Thanks to you for your kindness, your generous spirit, and the care you always show. Thanks to you for your thoughtful ways and good deeds, for adding so much to everything you do. Just by being the wonderful person you are, you've made a day, a relationship, a life better. You've made a difference. Thanks to you.

Thanks to you for...

Love and kindness are never wasted.
They always make a difference.

Barbara De Angelis

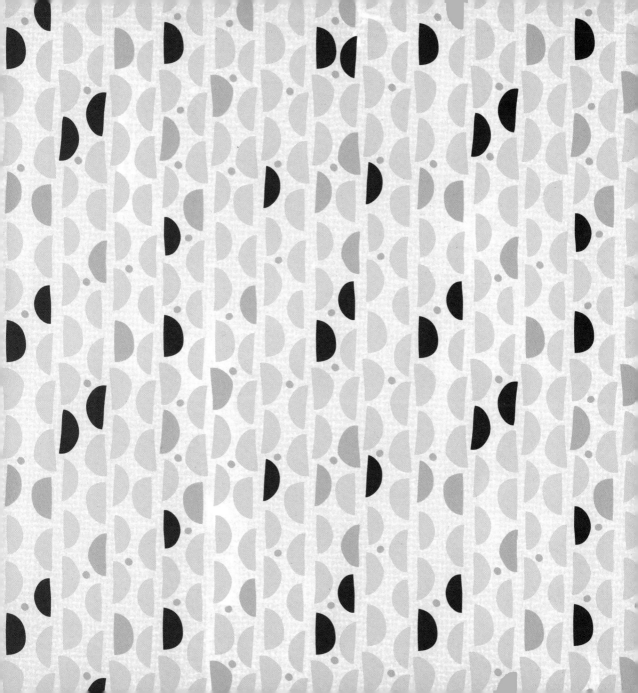

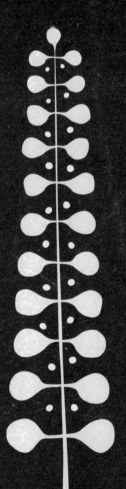

*Anything that has real
and lasting value is always
a gift from within.*

Franz Kafka

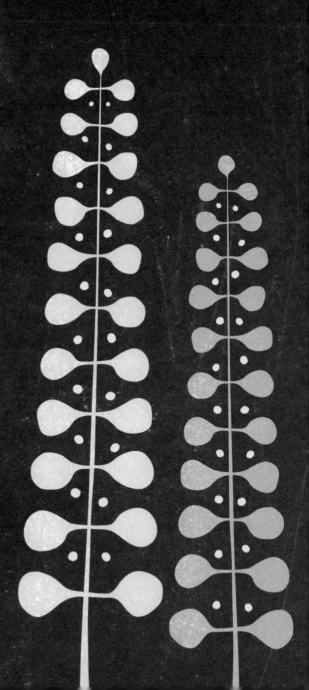

*Kindness is the
greatest wisdom.*

Unknown

Happiness is a by-product of an effort to make someone else happy.

Gretta Brooker Palmer

Three things in human life are
important: the first is to be kind;
the second is to be kind;
and the third is to be kind.

Henry James

Guard well within yourself that treasure, kindness...

George Sand

As we work to create light for others,
we naturally light our own way.

Mary Anne Radmacher

Kind people are the best
kind of people.

Unknown

Thanks to you for...

Your
Thoughtful
Ways

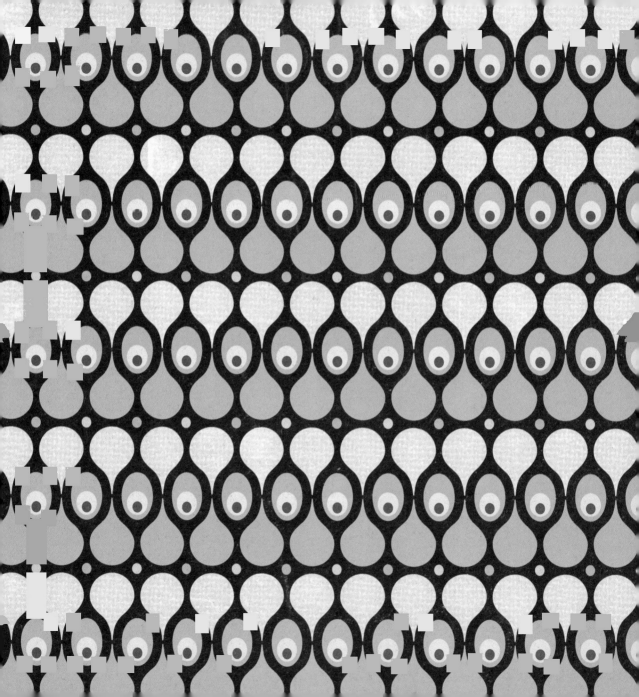

A little consideration,
a little thought for others,
makes all the difference.

A. A. Milne

A good deed is never lost.

Saint Basil the Great

Giving connects two people,
the giver and the receiver,
and this connects us all
to a new sense of belonging.

Deepak Chopra

There is no exercise better for the heart than reaching down and lifting people up.

John Holmes

No act of kindness is too small. The gift of kindness may start as a small ripple that over time can turn into a tidal wave affecting the lives of many.

Kevin Heath

• • • • • • • • • •

*It's not how much we give
but how much love
we put into giving.*

Mother Teresa

Thanks to you for...

the Care You Always Show

▭ ● ▭

Each smallest act of
kindness reverberates across great
distances and spans of time…
Because kindness is passed on and grows
each time it's passed until a simple
courtesy becomes an act of selfless
courage, years later, and far away.

Dean Koontz

If… there be any kindness
I can show, or any good thing
I can do to any fellow
human being, let me do it now.

Quaker Saying

I feel the capacity to care
is the thing which gives life
its deepest significance.

Pablo Casals

Having a sense of caring,
a feeling of compassion
will bring happiness of
peace of mind to oneself...

Dalai Lama

Live simply, love generously,
care deeply, speak kindly…

Ronald Reagan

*Caring about others, running
the risk of feeling, and leaving an
impact on people, brings happiness.*

Harold Kushner

Thanks to you for...

Your Generosity

I have found that there is a tremendous joy in giving. It is a very important part of the joy of living.

William Black

Happiness exists on earth,
and it is won through…[the]
constant practice of generosity.

José Martí

You will receive abundance
for your giving.
The more you give,
the more you will have!

W. Clement Stone

Sometimes when we are generous in small,
barely detectable ways
it can change someone's life forever.

Margaret Cho

*It is when you give of
yourself that you truly give.*

Kahlil Gibran

Every action generates positive energy
which can be shared with others.
These qualities of caring
and responsiveness
are the greatest gift
we can offer.

Tarthang Tulku

To generous souls every task is noble.

Euripides

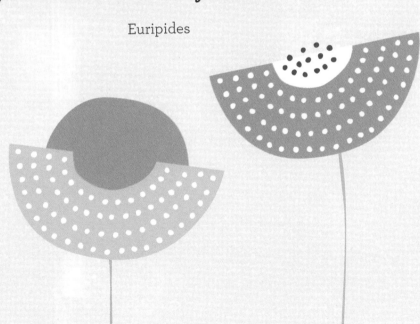

Do all the good you can,
by all the means you can...

John Wesley

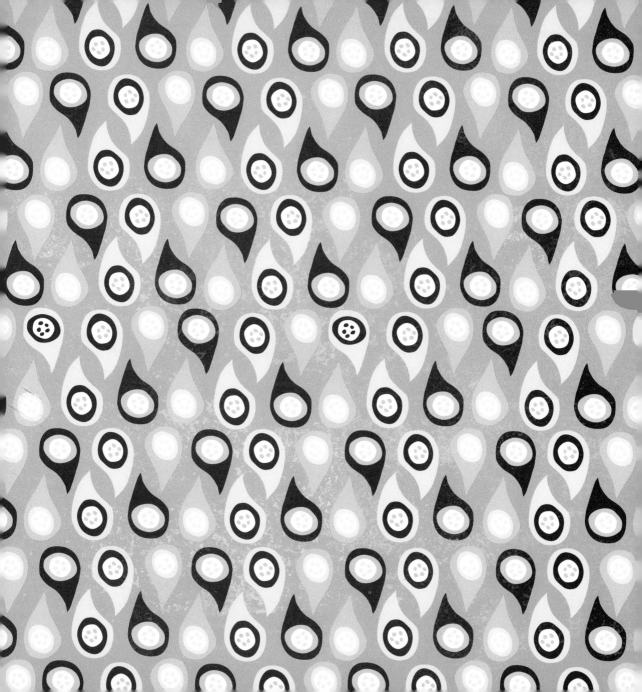

Thanks to you for...

Give yourself entirely to those around you. Be generous with your blessings.

Steve Maraboli

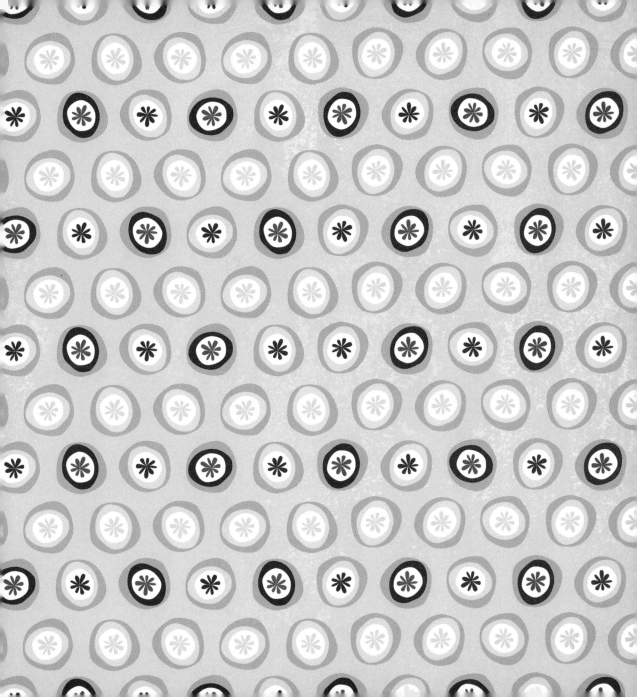

Too often we underestimate
the power of a touch, a smile,
a kind word, a listening ear,
an honest compliment, or
the smallest act of caring,
all of which have the potential
to turn a life around.

Leo Buscaglia

*Every day we're given
small opportunities to
bring someone joy...*

Delilah

*Good people increase the
value of every other person...*

Kelly Ann Rothaus

Thanks to you for...

Your good Heart

*We must not only give
what we have, we must
also give what we are.*

Cardinal Mercier

*The language of the heart
is the only language that
everybody can understand.*

Sri Chinmoy

The happy heart gives away the best.

Dhyani Ywahoo

*There are moments when
the heart is generous, and then
it knows that for better or worse our
lives are woven together here,
one with one another and with the
place and all the living things.*

Wendell Berry

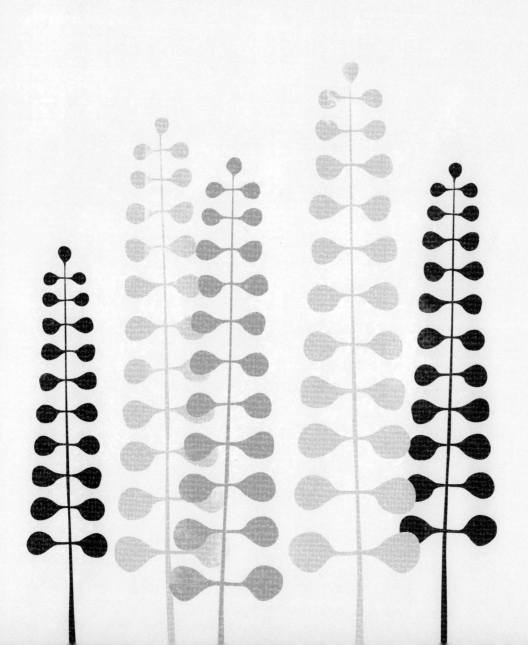

Open hearts will open more hearts.

Cat Forsley

When we give cheerfully
and accept gratefully,
everyone is blessed.

Maya Angelou

Thanks to you for...

Making a Difference

COMPENDIUM®
live inspired.

With special thanks to the entire Compendium family.

Credits:

Written & Compiled by: Amelia Riedler

Designed by: Steve Potter

Edited by: M.H. Clark

Creative Direction by: Julie Flahiff

ISBN: 978-1-938298-05-9

1st printing. Printed in China with soy inks.